CAMBRIDGE
UNIVERSITY PRESS

Cambridge Lower Secondary
Science

ENGLISH LANGUAGE SKILLS WORKBOOK 9

Mary Jones & Sally Burbeary

CAMBRIDGE
UNIVERSITY PRESS

University Printing House, Cambridge CB2 8BS, United Kingdom

One Liberty Plaza, 20th Floor, New York, NY 10006, USA

477 Williamstown Road, Port Melbourne, VIC 3207, Australia

314–321, 3rd Floor, Plot 3, Splendor Forum, Jasola District Centre, New Delhi – 110025, India

103 Penang Road, #05–06/07, Visioncrest Commercial, Singapore 238467

Cambridge University Press is part of the University of Cambridge.

It furthers the University's mission by disseminating knowledge in the pursuit of education, learning and research at the highest international levels of excellence.

www.cambridge.org
Information on this title: www.cambridge.org/9781108799065

First published 2014
Second edition 2021

20 19 18 17 16 15 14 13 12 11 10 9 8 7 6 5 4 3

Printed in Poland by Opolgraf

A catalogue record for this publication is available from the British Library

ISBN 978-1-108-79906-5 Paperback with Digital Access (1 year)

Cambridge International copyright material in this publication is reproduced under licence and remains the intellectual property of Cambridge Assessment International Education.

› Contents

English Skills and Support

1   Photosynthesis and the carbon cycle

2   Properties of materials

8 Rates of reaction

9 Electricity

> How to use this book

This workbook will help you to use and understand the English that is involved while learning science.

It will help you to:

*   understand what you read in your science books, and what your teacher tells you during the lessons

*   talk to other learners in your class in English, during your science lessons, using the correct vocabulary

*   understand questions that you are asked by your teacher or in tests

*   speak or write answers to science questions that say clearly what you mean.

This workbook contains an **English Skills and Support** section. This contains information about English grammar and vocabulary to help you with science. You can use the reference section at any time you need help with English while studying science.

Exercise 2

This exercise is about some of the vocabulary you have learnt in this topic.

Complete these sentences. Use some of these words.

| cells | chlorophyll | chloroplasts | fertiliser | photosynthesis |
| nitrate | root hairs | stomata | water | yield |

Plants make their own food by .... They absorb carbon dioxide from the air through the .... in their leaves. The carbon dioxide reacts with water inside the .... in the palisade cells in the leaf, forming glucose.

Plants can use the glucose that they make to produce other substances. For example, plants use .... from the soil to convert the glucose to proteins. They can also make .... , using magnesium from the soil.

This workbook provides questions for you to practise what you have learnt in class. There is a topic to match each topic in your Learner's Book and two Exercises in each Topic. You can use the English Skills and Support section to help you as you complete the Exercises.

Exercise 1

In this exercise, you will use an active verb to rewrite a sentence about how scientists think the Moon was formed. Look at the information about *active and passive verbs* in the English Skills and Support section.

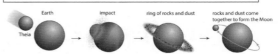
Earth · impact · ring of rocks and dust · rocks and dust come together to form the Moon · Theia

Each of these sentences includes a passive verb.

Underline the passive verb. Then rewrite the sentence using an active verb. You may also need to change some other words in the sentence so that it makes sense.

Here is an example.

> Rocks <u>were sent</u> flying into space when the collision happened.
>
> The collision sent rocks flying into space.

a   Dust and rocks were pulled together by gravity.

   ....

> English Skills and Support

This book is to help you with English skills when you are studying science. The English Skills and Support section gives you information about important topics in English that you will use in science. You can use this section at any time you need help with English while studying science.

You will see many different grammatical terms in the English language reference section explained.

Command words

Science questions often start with command words, for example, 'suggest', 'decide', 'evaluate' and 'explain'. You need to know how to answer these questions correctly.

Command words	Definition
Suggest	Give a possible reason why something happens or which method could be used.
Decide	To make a judgement based on different alternatives.
Evaluate	To assess the advantages and disadvantages of something, such as a scientific investigation.
Explain	Say **why** something happens.
Write down	This simply means write on paper.
Predict	To say that something will be or may be in the future.
Calculate	Work out mathematically. It is usually important to show your working in an organised way.

For example:

Question: **Suggest** how to measure the volume of an object.

Answer: Place the object in a measuring cylinder full of water and measure how much water is displaced.

Question: **Decide** what is wrong with this sentence, and underline the word that should be changed: The more dense a material, the more likely it is to float on water.

Answer: The word 'more' before dense should be underlined and replaced with 'less'.

Question: **Describe** how the intensity of light affects photosynthesis.

Answer: As light intensity increases, the rate of photosynthesis increases.

Question: **Explain** why the intensity of light affects photosynthesis.

Answer: Plants use energy in light for photosynthesis. The more light they have, the more energy they can use.

Question: **Write down** the result.

Answer: The water boiled at 100 degrees Celsius.

Question: **Predict** what will happen if you use a silver ring in an electrical circuit.

Answer: I think the silver ring will conduct the electricity.

Connecting words

Connecting words help you to join two pieces of information together in different ways.

In science, we often need to talk about more than one thing. We can join two ideas together with connecting words, for example: 'and', 'but', 'because', 'so'. These are called connectives. Connectives are like glue – they stick two ideas together.

There are many connecting words in English and they do different things in sentences.

Connective	What it is used for
and	Connects two positives together
but	Connects a positive and a negative together
because	Gives a reason why and is usually followed by a subject and a verb
because of	Gives a reason why and is usually followed by a verb ending in -ing or a noun.
so	Gives the result of a situation
as a result of	Effect + as a result of + cause
in order to	Action + in order to + purpose

Here are some examples.

and	*positive*	+	*positive*
	Iron is strong	and	hard.
but	*positive*	+	*negative*
	Iron is strong and hard	but	sodium is much softer.
because	*fact or situation*	+	*why*
	Countries agreed to reduce carbon dioxide emissions	because	they want to improve air quality.
because of	*fact or situation*	+	*why*
	Countries agreed to reduce carbon dioxide emissions	because of	global warming.
so	*fact or situation*	+	*result*
	Plants have roots	so	they can absorb minerals from the soil.
as a result of	Air quality has improved	as a result of	reducing carbon emissions.
in order to	We use a catalyst	in order to	increase the speed of the reaction.

The language of science experiments

When doing scientific experiments, you often use words such as 'observations', 'explanations', 'conclusions' and 'results'. You need to be clear what they mean and how to use them.

observe / observation	Meaning	To watch, smell, feel or hear what is happening during an experiment or investigation.
	Example	I made an observation that water became a solid at 0 degrees Celsius.
result	Meaning	A result is the raw data that you discover.
	Example	Two spoonfuls of sugar dissolved in the water, but only one spoonful of salt dissolved in the same volume of water.
conclude / conclusion	Meaning	This is at the end of the experiment when you have looked at all the results and make a decision, judgement or find a solution.
	Example	The conclusion of the experiment was that salt is less soluble than sugar.
explain / explanation	Meaning	This is when you explain why or how something happens.
	Example	This is my explanation. The oil floated on the water because the density of oil is less than the density of water.
variable	Meaning	A variable is something that can be changed in an experiment. The **independent variable** is the thing that we change. The **dependent variable** is the thing that we measure to collect results. Other variables are **controlled variables**, which means they are kept the same.
	Example	If we want to investigate how light intensity affects the rate at which bubbles of oxygen are produced by a water plant, we change the light intensity (independent variable), record the number of bubbles produced per minute at each value of the light intensity (dependent variable) and keep temperature, size of plant, species of plant and so on the same (controlled variables).

accurate / inaccurate / accuracy	Meaning	Accuracy is how close a measured value is to the actual (true) value.
	Example	A thermometer that is wrongly calibrated (the scale not marked correctly) gives an inaccurate reading (the reading is not true). If the thermometer is correctly calibrated and you do not read it carefully, that also gives an inaccurate reading. To achieve accuracy, we need to use good-quality measuring instruments, with care. We can check for accuracy by measuring the same thing with more than one instrument – if they both give the same value, then you can be more confident that this value is correct, or accurate.
precise / precision	Meaning	Precision is how close the measured values are to each other when you get the same reading for the same value on every occasion.
	Example	If you get the same temperature readings on a thermometer every time, then these readings are precise – but this does not always mean that the readings are the true value. You can be precise by using the measuring instrument correctly and with care, and taking the reading more than once to check that you get the same reading each time.
reliable / unreliable / reliability	Meaning	Reliability is how much we trust the results. If results are reliable, we should get the same ones if we do the same experiment in the same way again.
	Example	I have repeated this experiment three times in exactly the same way and the results were the same every time. I think the results are reliable.
trend	Meaning	Trend refers to the overall 'direction' a set of data is going in.
	Example	The trend is, as time increases, the temperature of the beaker of hot water decreases.

pattern	Meaning	A pattern is something that repeats in a predictable way in a set of data.
	Example	There is a general trend that carbon dioxide levels in the atmosphere are increasing. There is a pattern that these fall slightly in the summer and rise slightly in the winter. This is because plants take carbon dioxide from the air when they photosynthesise, which they do more in summer.
hypothesis	Meaning	A hypothesis is an idea or explanation that is based on scientific understanding, and can be tested by experiment. It is usually presented as a statement, often saying how we think that changing one variable will affect another.
	Example	Plants need water to survive. This would be disproved if you find a plant that does not need water. A hypothesis does not have to be correct – the experiment will discover whether it is correct or not.
support a hypothesis	Meaning	If your results match what the hypothesis predicted, then we say that they 'support the hypothesis'. We cannot say that they 'prove' it. You have to do many different experiments to prove a hypothesis.
	Example	After several experiments, the plants I didn't water eventually died. So, the results support the hypothesis that 'plants need water to survive'.
refute a hypothesis	Meaning	When your results do not match what the hypothesis predicted, the hypothesis is refuted (found to be wrong). You cannot be sure with just one experiment; you would want to do it again to check. It is much easier to disprove a hypothesis than to prove one!
	Example	Hypothesis: Adding $50\,cm^3$ of water to plants each day helps them grow, so adding $100\,cm^3$ of water each day will make them grow even more. If you did an experiment to test this hypothesis, it would be refuted because you would probably find that some plants do not need that much water. If the soil a plant is in has too much water, the roots can rot.

theory	Meaning	A theory is a scientific idea that has a lot of evidence supporting it – many experiments have shown again and again that the theory is supported.
	Example	The theory of plate tectonics (the movement of seven large plates on planet Earth) explains how mountains are formed. Scientists noticed on a map that some of Earth's continents look as though they could 'fit together' like a jigsaw, but they are separated by water. The theory of plate tectonics explains these observations. Many other observations can also be explained by this theory.
risk assessment	Meaning	Risk assessment is thinking in advance about any risks or hazards that might arise while doing an experiment or other activity. Each potential risk is identified, and a decision is made about how to keep the risk to a minimum.
	Example	My risk assessment showed that during this experiment, acid could contact my skin. I will wear protective clothing and handle the acid with care to minimise the risk.
hazard / hazardous	Meaning	A hazard is a part of a scientific practical experiment that could cause harm or a health and safety risk. You should be able to identify hazards and take measures to reduce the risk that they pose.
	Example	A hazard of using acids is that if the acid gets onto your skin, it will burn you.
limit / limitations	Meaning	Limitations are reasons why we cannot be sure that a conclusion is correct.
	Example	I measured the heights of four learners and found that the two boys were taller than the two girls. I could make a conclusion that boys are taller than girls, but this conclusion has many limitations because I only have four measurements. I need to take many more measurements in order to make a conclusion that has fewer limitations.

	Meaning	A model is a way of representing a concept (idea) or structure by one that is much easier to understand.
model	Example	You can represent the lungs and the diaphragm using a balloon inside a bell jar and you can use this model to show how movement of the diaphragm causes air to move into the lungs. glass tube stopper bell jar air balloons rubber sheet before the rubber sheet is pulled after the rubber sheet is pulled
analogy	Meaning	An analogy compares one concept, structure or system with another, to explain the concept clearly.
	Example	You can use the Solar System as an analogy for the structure of an atom. The Solar System has the Sun at its centre, while the atom has a nucleus. Planets orbit around the Sun, whereas electrons orbit around the nucleus of the atom. Analogies are never perfect.
unit	Meaning	A unit is the quantity in which a measurement is made.
	Example	Which unit should we use to measure the speed of the reaction, in seconds or minutes?

Modal verbs

Modal verbs are a special type of verb that go before other verbs in a sentence. Modal verbs show that things are *certain*, *probable*, *possible* or *impossible*.

There are many modal verbs and each one has a different function or functions.

Here are some of the common modal verbs.

can	This modal verb shows: • an **ability** to do something • that something is **possible**.
Species **can** adapt to their changing habitats. (Species have the **ability** to adapt.) Water **can** transform into a gas. (It is **possible** for water to transform into a gas.)	
cannot (can't)	This means the opposite. It means: • you are **not able** to do something • that something is **not possible**.
Whales **cannot** survive on land. (Whales do **not** have the **ability** to survive on land.) Coral reefs **can't** grow if the water is cloudy. (It is **not possible** for coral reefs to grow if the water is cloudy.)	

must	This is a strong modal verb and it means that something is **mandatory** (you **can't** say no).
You **must** check your equipment is calibrated correctly if you want your results to be accurate. (It is essential to do this, to ensure your results are accurate.)	
must not (mustn't)	This means the opposite. It means that it is mandatory **not** to do something.
You **must not** use acids without wearing goggles. (It is essential not to do this as it is very dangerous.)	

should	Use this modal verb to: • give **advice** • show something you **expect** will happen.
You **should** repeat experiments to reduce limitations. (I **advise** you to do this.) Water **should** evaporate more quickly at higher temperatures. (You **expect** water to evaporate at higher temperatures.)	
should not (shouldn't)	This means the opposite. It means: • **advise not** to do something • something that you **do not expect** to happen.
You **should not** smoke. (I **advise** you **not** to do this.) Wood **should not** conduct electricity. (You **do not expect** wood to conduct electricity.)	

Comparative adjectives and adverbs and superlative adjectives

This topic helps you to do *two* things. It helps you to talk about:

1 the differences between things (comparative adjectives and adverbs)

2 the upper and lower limits of something (superlative adjectives).

Scientists often want to compare two or more things. For example:

• feathers and leaves are *lighter* than stones and rocks. (comparative adjective)

• evaporation occurs *more quickly* at higher temperatures. (comparative adverb)

Comparative adjectives

Comparative adjectives describe similarities and differences between two or more nouns. They are formed by adding *-er* to shorter adjectives and *more* before longer adjectives.

Comparative adjectives		
You make a <u>comparative adjective</u> by adding **-er** to the end of short adjectives. This rule works with adjectives that have 1 syllable (sound), 2 syllable adjectives ending in 'y, er, le and ow.'		
adjective	comparative	Example sentence
small	small<u>er</u>	Atoms are <u>smaller</u> than molecules.
cloudy	cloud<u>ier</u>	The liquid turned <u>cloudier</u> when more sugar was added.
simple	simpl<u>er</u>	This method was <u>simpler</u> to understand.

Comparative adjectives	
You make a <u>comparative adjective</u> by adding **more** before long adjectives. This rule works with 2 syllable adjectives not ending in 'y, er, le and ow' and adjectives with 3 syllables or more.	
more + adjective	Example sentence
more helpful	This explanation is <u>more helpful</u> than the other one.
more flexible	A ball and socket joint is <u>more flexible</u> than a hinge joint.
more acidic	Vinegar is <u>more acidic</u> than milk.

Spelling rules when forming comparative adjectives.

	Adjective + er	
1 syllable adjectives ending in 2 consonants	long	longer
1 syllable adjectives ending in 2 vowels and one consonant	weak	weaker
When the last 3 letters are consonant, vowel, consonant, you must double the last letter	big flat	bigger flatter
When the adjective ends in 'y' take off the 'y' and add -ier.	busy	busier
When the adjective end in 'e' just add -r.	safe	safer

Structure of comparative sentences

Noun + verb + adjective + er + than + noun.

Comparatives	Other notes about the sentence
A <u>silver ring</u> is *shinier* than an iron nail.	(singular countable noun + is)
<u>Carbon dioxide gas</u> is *heavier* than oxygen.	(uncountable noun + is)
<u>Metals</u> are *stronger* than plastics.	(plural noun + are)
<u>Arctic hares</u> have *longer* ears than brown hares.	(you do not always have to use 'is' or 'are')

Noun + verb + more + adjective + than + noun.

Comparatives	Other notes about the sentence
A <u>lemon</u> is *more acidic* than milk.	(singular countable noun + is)
<u>Sugar</u> is *more soluble* in water than salt.	(uncountable noun + is)
<u>Tigers</u> are *more aggressive* than lions.	(plural noun + are)
<u>Brick</u> has a *greater density* than water.	(you do not always have to use 'is' or 'are')

You can compare two things that have the same properties by saying, 'as + adjective + as,' for example, 'Vinegar is *as acidic as* lemon juice. Neptune is *as cold as* Uranus.'.

Comparative adverbs

Adverbs describe how, when, how often, or to what degree an action is done. Most adverbs end in -ly, for example, 'quickly', 'brightly', 'safely'.

Comparative adverbs make comparisons between two verbs. To form comparative adverbs, add -er to the end of 1 syllable adverbs, for example: hard – harder, fast – faster. Most adverbs are two-syllable words, ending in -ly, so you will usually use 'more' in front of the adverb to compare two actions. For example: 'more slowly' and 'more carefully'.

- Humans can run fast, but cheetahs can run more quickly.
- Ice melts at room temperature, but ice melts more slowly at low temperatures.
- We got the results more quickly this lesson, compared with last week.
- The chemical reaction happened faster than I expected.
- I study harder than him.
- Eagles fly higher than crows.

Superlative adjectives

In science, we also want to say what is at the top or the bottom of a range of things. Superlative adjectives say what is at the top and the bottom of a range.

Remember, you make a superlative adjective by adding:

- *-est* to the end of short adjectives (hard, cold, large, small).
  For example: The blue whale is *the largest* marine mammal on Earth.
- 'the most' before longer adjectives (reactive, conductive, reflective).
  For example: White is *the most reflective* colour.

Be careful! Words of two syllables (sounds) can use both *-est* and 'the most'.

For two-syllable adjectives ending in 'y', add *-est* (heavy – the heaviest).

For adjectives of two or more syllables **not** ending in 'y', add 'the most' before the adjective (active – *the most* active; reactive – *the most* reactive).

Notice that you always put 'the' before superlative adjectives.

Be aware that some adjectives are irregular. This means they do not follow the usual rules.

Irregular adjectives		
Adjective	Comparative	Superlative
far	further	the furthest
few	fewer	the least
little	less	the least
many	more	the most

Phrasal verbs

Phrasal verbs are mostly made up of a verb followed by a preposition. Prepositions are usually short words – for example: 'in', 'out', 'up', 'of', 'by', 'into'. Phrasal verbs are used a lot in English and science. Each phrase can have many meanings, but these are some common uses of phrasal verbs used in science. You could add more to the list if you meet some different ones.

Verbs used without a preposition have one meaning, for example 'work', but when you add a preposition to the verb it has a different meaning, for example, 'work out'.

		Meaning	Example
go	out	A fire or light stops shining or stops burning.	The fire will *go out* if I starve it of oxygen.
put	out	To extinguish (usually fire or light).	I *put out* the fire by covering it with a damp cloth.
work	out	To solve a problem or calculate the result.	I can *work out* if aluminium is conductive by connecting it to a circuit.
washed	up	Carry something on water until it lands on the beach or land.	Seaweed was *washed up* on the beach after the storm.
made	up of	Composed of – what is inside or included.	Salt is *made up of* two elements, sodium and chlorine.
divided	into	Create smaller groups.	Metals are *divided into* two categories.

The phrase 'can tell' is not a phrasal verb, but it is a useful phrase to know because it is used a lot in science. It means that something is noticeable. An example sentence is:

I can tell this plant has been over watered.

Graphs

You need to know the names of the different parts of a graph.

Here is a distance/time graph for a girl riding a bicycle.

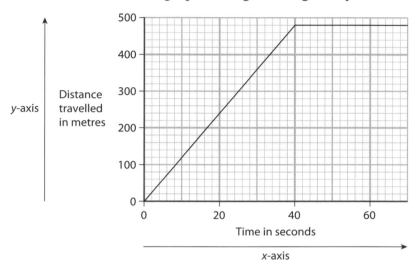

The line is **straight** and **sloping** upwards from 0 seconds to 40 seconds.

The line is **straight** and **horizontal** from 40 s to 60 s.

Turning verbs into nouns

We can turn many verbs into nouns by adding *-ion* or *-ment* to the end of the verb. When you add letters to the end of words, these are called suffixes.

Words ending in	Remove	Add	Example verbs	Example nouns
ate	the final 'e'	ion	separate illuminate formulate	separation illumination formulation
ise	the final 'e'	ation	globalise equalise immunise	globalisation equalisation immunisation
ode	the final 'de'	sion	corrode explode implode	corrosion explosion implosion

Words ending in	Remove	Add	Example verbs	Example nouns
ine	the final 'e'	ation *or* ition	examine imagine define	examination imagination definition
ct		ion	attract instruct obstruct	attraction instruction obstruction
er	the final 'er'	ration	administer filter	administration filtration
er		ation	alter consider	alteration consideration

Notice that verbs ending in *-er* have two rules. Also, note that all words ending in *-ate*, *-ise*, *-ode*, *-ine*, *-ct*, and *-er*, make a noun by adding **-ion**.

The verbs that take *-ment* at the end to make a noun have an easy spelling rule: just add **-ment** to the end.

Add	Example verbs	Example nouns
ment	develop improve nourish state	development improvement nourishment statement

Example sentences:

I would like to *separate* the particles by using a *filter*.

- The **separation** of particles is done by **filtration**.

Acid rain *corrodes* rocks.

- **Corrosion** happens when rocks are exposed to acid rain.

Opposite magnetic poles *attract*.

- Magnetic **attraction** is the opposite of magnetic repulsion.

I would like to *improve* this experiment.

- When I checked the calibration of the equipment, there was significant **improvement** of the results.

Prepositions

Prepositions are usually short words, for example: 'in', 'on', 'at', 'by', 'from'. Each preposition has a particular meaning and it is important that you know how they are used in sentences.

'In', 'at' and 'on' are very common prepositions. You can use them to talk about time or place. Here are some examples of how they are used to talk about place.

Prepositions – place	Usage	Examples
in	Within a space or area, or inside something.	in a town/country in the water in a school (inside the building) in the centre
at	A point or particular place.	at my desk at the top/bottom at school (at this place)
on	A surface.	my book is on the table wood floats on water on the floor

Prepositions	Usage	Examples
through	Moving from one end to the other, in something.	Electricity flows *through* copper wire. Blood travels *through* the body.
from	Comes *from* a source.	Metal ore is extracted *from* rocks. Arteries carry blood away *from* the heart.
into	Indicates movement towards the inside of a place.	Light comes *into* the room. Water flows *into* the river.
made up of	Consists or has these parts inside.	A water molecule is *made up of* two hydrogen atoms and one oxygen atom.
between	In the middle of and separates two things. Indicates the connection linking two things.	The Earth is *between* Venus and Mars. The similarity *between* magnesium and calcium is that they are both shiny and silvery-white.

Prepositions	Usage	Examples
by	Shows who or what caused the action or situation.	The experiment was conducted *by* the students. The explosion was caused *by* mixing chemicals.
with	links something *with* something else	magnesium reacts *with* oxygen to create magnesium oxide
without	indicates the lack of something in the described context	photosynthesis cannot take place *without* sunlight

Active and passive

You will see sentences using **active verbs** and **passive verbs** in science.

Active verbs

Use active verbs in sentences to give direct information.

Structure: Who does/did what.

Examples:
- I carried out the experiment.
- He calibrated the thermometer.
- She recorded the temperature accurately.

Passive verbs

Sometimes you need to use passive verbs. When the verb is passive, the subject has the action done to it, rather than the subject doing it.

Structure: Something is/are/was/were done by whom or what. It is possible to not include who did the action if who did it is not important.

Examples:
- The experiment was carried out (by me).
- The thermometer was calibrated (by him).
- The temperature was recorded accurately (by her).

Changing active to passive

Tense	Active		
	Who/what	verb	What
Simple present	I/you/we/they	**heat**	the liquid.
Simple present	She/he/it	**heats**	the liquid.
Verb form	Passive		
	what	is/are + past participle	Who/what
Past participle	The liquid	**is heated**	(by them).
Past participle	The liquids	**are heated**	(by us).

Notice how the word order changes when you change active to passive.

Conditional sentences

Conditional sentences show the result of conditions. Conditional sentences have an *if-clause*, that shows the condition, and a *main clause*, that shows the result. There are four types of conditional sentences, here we will look at zero conditional and first conditional sentences.

A zero conditional sentence shows facts or things that are generally true. It has two present simple verbs (one in the 'if clause' and one in the 'main clause').

If + present simple, ... present simple. For example:

If water reaches 100 degrees, it boils.

If you mix hydrogen and oxygen, you get water.

You can reverse the two clauses, for example:

Water boils if it reaches 100 degrees.

You get water if you mix hydrogen and oxygen.

Notice that when you start with the main clause, you don't need to use a comma.

First conditional sentences are used to talk about future situations that you think are possible.

The first conditional structure is: *if / when* + present simple ... *will* + infinitive.

If I study hard, I will pass my science exam.

If I leave the plant seeds for a week, I will see green shoots.

1 ▶ Photosynthesis and the carbon cycle

> 1.1 Photosynthesis

Exercise 1

This exercise checks that you can respond correctly to the words 'state', 'describe' and 'explain'. Look at the information about command words in the English Skills and Support section to help you to answer these questions.

The diagram shows some apparatus that Zara used to investigate the production of bubbles of gas by a water plant.

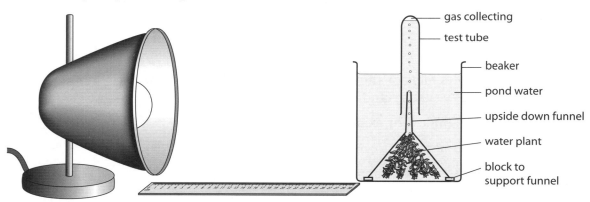

a   **State** the name of the process happening in the plant that produces the bubbles of gas.

   ....

b   **Describe** what happens during the process you have named in **a**.

   ....

   ....

   ....

c **State** the name of the green substance contained in plant cells that helps them to carry out this process.

....

d **Explain** why this green substance is needed.

....

....

....

e Zara used the apparatus to investigate the effect of changing the light intensity on the rate at which bubbles were produced.

Describe how she can vary the light intensity.

....

....

Exercise 2

This exercise is about using connecting words to link two ideas together.

Complete each sentence, using these connecting words or phrases. Sometimes, more than one word or phrase will fit – just choose the one you think is best.

and	**as a result of**	**because**	**because of**
but	**in order to**	**so**	

a Plants produce oxygen .... photosynthesis.

b Plants are green .... they contain chlorophyll.

c Plants need carbon dioxide .... water .... make oxygen and glucose.

d The light intensity received by this plant is high, ... it is photosynthesising rapidly.

e Plants do not photosynthesise at night .... it is dark.

> 1.2 More about photosynthesis

Exercise 1

In this exercise, you will practise using some words associated with scientific experiments. Look at the information about vocabulary for scientific experiments in the English Skills and Support section, to help you to answer these questions.

Marcus tests a leaf for starch.

a   This is one of the steps in his experiment.

What **hazard** does Marcus need to think about as he does this experiment?

....

b   Marcus takes the leaf out of the hot water and puts it into a tube containing ethanol. He stands the tube of ethanol in the beaker of hot water.

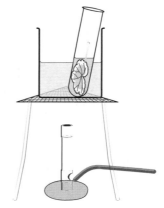

Describe the **observation** that Marcus will make when the leaf is in the hot ethanol.

....

....

c   Marcus takes the leaf out of the ethanol, rinses it in water and places it on a white tile.

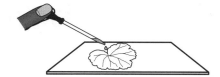

He adds iodine solution to it. The leaf goes blue-black.

i   What is Marcus's **observation**?

....

ii   What **conclusion** can Marcus make?

....

Exercise 2

This exercise is about some of the vocabulary you have learnt in this topic.

Complete these sentences. Use some of these words.

**cells   chlorophyll   chloroplasts   fertiliser   photosynthesis
nitrate   root hairs   stomata   water   yield**

Plants make their own food by .... They absorb carbon dioxide

from the air through the .... in their leaves. The carbon dioxide

reacts with water inside the .... in the palisade cells in the leaf,

forming glucose.

Plants can use the glucose that they make to produce other

substances. For example, plants use .... from the soil to convert

the glucose to proteins. They can also make .... , using

magnesium from the soil.

Farmers often add .... to the soil, to give crop plants more of

the minerals that they need. This can increase the .... that the

farmers get from the crops.

> 1.3 The carbon cycle

Exercise 1

In this exercise, you will practise turning statements into questions.

Change each statement into at least one question. Write more than one question if you can, but try not to ask anything that cannot be answered by reading the statement.

The first one has been done for you.

Statement: Plants take carbon dioxide from the air to use in photosynthesis.

Questions:

- Do plants take carbon dioxide from the air to use in photosynthesis?

- Which gas do plants take from the air to use in photosynthesis?

- Where do plants take carbon dioxide from, to use in photosynthesis?

- Why do plants need to take carbon dioxide from the air?

a *Statement*: Decomposers are important in the carbon cycle because they break down carbon compounds in other living things.

   Questions: ....

   ....

   ....

   ....

b *Statement*: All organisms release carbon dioxide when they respire.

   Questions: ....

   ....

   ....

   ....

c   *Statement*: The combustion of fossil fuels adds carbon dioxide to the air.

   Questions: ....

   ....

   ....

   ....

d   *Statement*: Fossil fuels formed from organisms that died millions of years ago.

   Questions: ....

   ....

   ....

   ....

Exercise 2

This exercise is about modal verbs. Look at the information about modal verbs in the English Skills and Support section to help you to answer these questions.

Complete each sentence, using the words that you think fit best.

Choose from the list.

can   **cannot**   **must**   **must not**

should   **should not**

a   Fossil fuels are non-renewable resources, so we .... try not to use too many of them.

b   When we do experiments with animals, we .... treat them with respect.

c   If we destroyed all of the plants on Earth, there .... be anything to remove carbon dioxide from the air.

d   Decomposers .... get carbon from every kind of living organism.

e   Living organisms .... use carbon in the form of an element.

f Now write a sentence using one of the words in the list that you have **not** used in your answers to **a**, **b**, **c** or **d**. Your sentence should include some information about the carbon cycle.

....

....

....

› 1.4 Climate change

Exercise 1

This exercise is about comparative adjectives and adverbs. Look at the information on comparative adjectives and adverbs in the English Skills and Support section to help you to answer these questions.

Choose the best comparative adjective or adverb to complete each sentence.

faster   greater   higher   larger   lower

more frequently   more slowly   smaller

a Snow turns to slush as the temperature gets ....

b Meteoroids are .... than asteroids.

c When a meteor enters the Earth's atmosphere, friction with the air makes it

travel ....

d As the Earth's mean temperature increases, the volume of water in the oceans

becomes ....

e Scientists think that extreme weather events will happen ....

as global warming continues.

Exercise 2

In this exercise, you will use phrases to complete sentences about the causes and effects of climate change.

Here are some phrases about climate change.

- **increase in the Earth's mean temperature**
- **mass extinction**
- **rise in sea level**
- **asteroid collision**

Use these phrases, and your own words, to complete the sentences.

Try to use all four phrases at least once.

a Global warming ....

....

....

b 67 million years ago ....

....

....

c Cities on coastlines, such as Los Angeles and Shanghai, ...

....

....

....

2 ▶ Properties of materials

❯ 2.1 Atomic structure and the Periodic Table

Exercise 1

This exercise asks you to think about the words **model** and **analogy**. You can find information about the meanings of these two words in the English Skills and Support section. You will also practise using some of the vocabulary that you have learnt in this topic.

The diagram shows a model of a lithium atom.

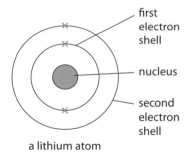

first electron shell

nucleus

second electron shell

a lithium atom

a Explain why we say that this diagram shows a **model** of an atom.

....

....

....

....

b Arun says that we can use the structure of the Solar System as an **analogy** to help us to think about the structure of an atom.

Describe **one** similarity and one difference between the structure of the Solar System and the structure of an atom.

Similarity: ....

....

Difference: ....

....

c In which electron shell of this atom do the electrons have a higher energy level?

....

d The electron shells are concentric. Explain what 'concentric' means.

....

....

e What do we call the forces that hold the electrons in place in their shells? Circle the correct words.

electoral forces   electrical forces   electrostatic forces

Exercise 2

This exercise is about the Periodic Table of the elements, and some of the vocabulary that we use to describe it.

The diagram shows part of the Periodic Table.

1 H hydrogen 1																	2 He helium 4
3 Li lithium 7	4 Be beryllium 9											5 B boron 11	6 C carbon 12	7 N nitrogen 14	8 O oxygen 16	9 F fluorine 19	10 Ne neon 20
11 Na sodium 23	12 Mg magnesium 24											13 Al aluminium 27	14 Si silicon 28	15 P phosphorus 31	16 S sulfur 32	17 Cl chlorine 35	18 Ar argon 40
19 K potassium 39	20 Ca calcium 40																

Look at the Periodic Table.

a   What is the mass number of lithium? ....

b   What is the atomic number of lithium? ....

c   Use a pencil to shade one group in the diagram of the Periodic Table.

d   What happens to the mass number of the elements as you go down the group you have shaded?

   ....

e   What happens to the number of protons in the nucleus of an atom, as you go down the group you have shaded?

   ....

f   The electronic structure of an atom is 2,4. It contains 6 neutrons.
   Draw a diagram to show this atom.
   Show the electrons in the correct electron shells.

> 2.2 Trends in groups within the Periodic Table

Exercise 1

In this exercise, you will practise using superlative adjectives and adverbs to describe trends in the Periodic Table.

The diagram shows the Periodic Table, with two groups shaded.

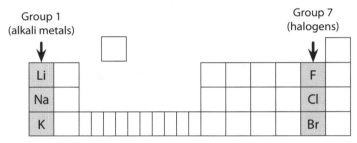

Look at the Group 1 metals.

a Write the symbol of the Group 1 metal with the greatest mass number.

....

b Write the name of the Group 1 metal that reacts most quickly with water.

....

Now look at the halogens. Complete these sentences.

Choose from the list.

highest   higher   least   lowest   lower   most

c Fluorine is the halogen with the .... atomic number.

d Bromine is the .... reactive of these three elements.

e Chlorine has a .... boiling point than fluorine.

> 2.3 Why elements react to form compounds

Exercise 1

> This exercise gives you practice in writing complete sentences, as well as thinking hard about how compounds are formed.

Here are some phrases about why elements react to form compounds.

is called a molecule	attracted to each other by ionic bonds
when the outermost electron shell is full	a covalent bond is formed
held together by chemical bonds	when an atom loses or gains electrons

Use each phrase to complete one of the sentences.

a   Atoms are most stable ....

....

b   An ion is formed ....

....

c   In a compound, atoms are ....

....

d   When atoms share electrons, we say that ....

....

e   The ions in an ionic compound are ....

....

f   A group of atoms held together by covalent bonds ....

....

Exercise 2

In this exercise, you will check that you can use some of the new vocabulary you have learnt in this topic. You will also practise answering questions that begin with different command words. Look at the information about command words in the English Skills and Support section, to help you to answer these questions.

The dot and cross diagram shows the structure of a molecule.

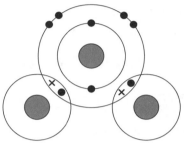

a   Name the two elements in this molecule.

....

b   Write down the chemical formula for this molecule.

....

c   State what the dots and crosses represent in this molecule.

dots: ....

crosses: ....

d   In this molecule, the atoms share electrons.
Name the type of bond in which atoms share electrons.

....

e   Explain why this molecule is a compound, not an element.

....

....

....

f   Name this compound.

....

> 2.4 Simple and giant structures

Exercise 1

> This exercise gives you practice in using some of the new words you have learnt in this topic.

a Complete the sentences about an ionic compound that forms a giant structure. Choose words from the list.

compound   lattice   molecule   negative   positive

Sodium chloride is a .... containing sodium ions and chloride

ions. Each sodium ion has a .... charge and each chloride ion

has a .... charge.

These opposite charges mean that the sodium ions and chloride ions are

strongly attracted to one another, forming ionic bonds. Millions of sodium

ions and chloride ions form a giant structure called a ....

b Complete the sentences about an element that forms a giant covalent structure. Choose words from the list.

aeroplanes   atoms   easily   ions   covalent
ionic   pencil leads   stronger   weaker

Graphite is a form of carbon in which the carbon .... are

arranged in layers. In each layer, many carbon atoms form strong

.... bonds with each other, by sharing electrons.

There are .... bonds between the layers. This means that the

layers can .... slide over one another.

This makes graphite very soft, which is why it is good for making

....

Exercise 2

In this exercise, you will complete sentences using comparative words that you choose for yourself. You may like to look at the information about comparative adjectives and adverbs in the English Skills and Support section.

These sentences compare the properties of ionic compounds and covalent compounds. Complete the sentences, using your own choice of comparative adjectives or comparative adverbs.

a   Covalent compounds usually have .... boiling points than ionic compounds.

b   Ionic compounds dissolve in water .... than covalent compounds.

c   Ionic compounds have .... melting points than covalent compounds. This is because the electrostatic forces that hold the ions together

     are .... than the intermolecular forces that hold the

     molecules together in a covalent compound.

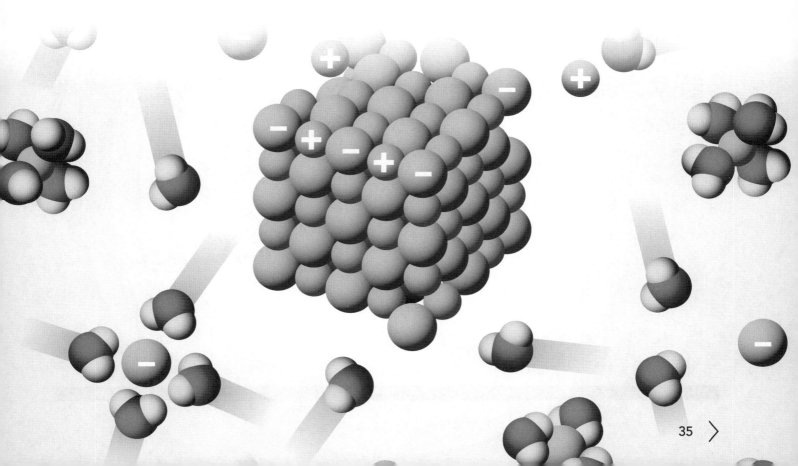

Forces and energy

> 3.1 Density

Exercise 1

This exercise is about some of the two-word phrases that we use in science. You can find information about many different two-word phrases in the English Skills and Support section.

Choose one of these two-word phrases to complete each sentence. You can use each phrase once, more than once or not at all.

go out   put out   washed up   work out

a   We can .... the density of an object by dividing its mass by its volume.

b   Oil is less dense than water, so an oil spill

floats and can be ....
onto a beach.

c   Carbon dioxide gas is more dense than air,

air, so we can .... a fire by pouring carbon dioxide onto it, which prevents oxygen in the air from reaching the fire.

d   We can .... the volume of an irregular object by measuring the volume of water it displaces.

Exercise 2

> This exercise is about writing sentences that use connecting words. You can find information about connecting words in the English Skills and Support section.

Write a sentence about each of the following ideas. Use one of these connecting words in each of your sentences. You might be able to use more than one of them in some of your sentences.

because   **but**   **so**

The first one has been done for you.

Idea: the difference in density between gases and liquids

Gases have a lower density than liquids **because** their particles are further apart.

a *Idea*: how we can find the volume of a regular and an irregular object

....

....

....

b *Idea*: the difference in density between a solid piece of iron and a hollow piece of iron

....

....

....

c *Idea*: the effect on density of compressing a gas and a solid

....

....

....

d *Idea*: what makes a hot air balloon float

....

....

....

> 3.2 Heat and temperature

Exercise 1

> In this exercise, you will complete sentences about the difference between heat (thermal energy) and temperature.

Complete each sentence. Choose words from the list.

average   greater   less   more   smaller   total

a   The higher the temperature of a liquid, the

.... the energy of its particles.

b   Temperature tells us about the

.... energy of particles.

c   Heat tells us about the .... energy of particles.

d   The more thermal energy we add to a liquid,

the .... its temperature increases.

e   A large volume of water with a temperature

of 60°C has a .... quantity quantity of thermal energy than a smaller volume of water with a temperature of 60°C.

Exercise 2

In this exercise, you will write your own questions about heat and temperature and then answer them.

Write a question about each of these topics. Your question should be a complete sentence.

Then write an answer to your question. The answer does not need to be a complete sentence.

The first one has been done for you.

measuring temperature

Question: What instrument do we use to measure the temperature of an object?

Answer: A thermometer.

a thermal energy transfers between two objects at different temperatures

Question: ....

....

Answer: ....

....

b effect of adding thermal energy to a liquid

Question: ....

....

Answer: ....

....

c ice cream melting

Question: ....

....

Answer: ....

....

> 3.3 Conservation of energy

Exercise 1

This exercise asks you to correct some sentences about conservation of energy.

Two words in each of these sentences have swapped places.

In each sentence, draw circles round the two words that are in the wrong place. Then write the sentence with the words in their correct places.

a   Conserved is always energy.

....

b   The total energy input from a system cannot be greater than the total energy output.

....

....

c   When energy is transferred from one heat to another, some may be dissipated as system.

....

....

d   Energy cannot be changed or destroyed, only created from one form to another.

....

....

e   When 100 J of electrical energy is supplied to a system, the less output energy will be useful than 100 J.

....

....

Exercise 2

In this exercise, you will practise turning a statement into a question.

Change each statement into at least one question. Write more than one question if you can, but try not to ask anything that cannot be answered by reading the statement.

The first one has been done for you.

> *Statement*: A lamp changes 10 J of its input energy to light, but the remaining 90 J is changed to thermal energy.
>
> *Questions*: What is the total energy input to the lamp?
>
> What proportion of the energy provided to a lamp is changed to useful energy?

a   *Statement*: The law of conservation of energy states than energy cannot be created or destroyed.

   Questions: ....

   ....

   ....

   ....

b   *Statement*: The total quantity of energy that enters a system is the same as the total quantity of energy that leaves it.

   Questions: ....

   ....

   ....

   ....

c   *Statement*: If we put 100 J of energy into a system, we cannot get more than 100 J of energy out of it.

   Questions: ....

   ....

   ....

   ....

> 3.4 Moving from hot to cold

Exercise 1

In this exercise, you will choose comparative words of your own, to complete sentences. You can find information about comparative adjectives in the English Skills and Support section.

Use a comparative adjective to complete each sentence.

a   The temperature of your hands decreases when you hold an ice cube,

because the ice cube is .... than your hands.

b   A substance that is colder has a .... temperature.

c   Thermal energy moves to .... places.

d   The .... the difference in temperature between two places,
the faster the rate at which the thermal energy transfers from one to the other.

e   When cold water flows through the hot engine of a car, the water gets

....

Exercise 2

This exercise is about information shown in a graph. Look at the sections on command words and graphs in the English Skills and Support section to help you to answer these questions.

Arun put some hot water into a beaker. He measured the temperature of the water every 5 minutes for the next 40 minutes. The graph shows his results.

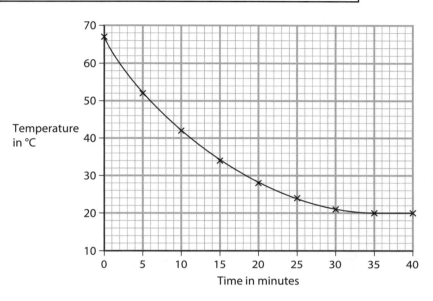

a What are the **units** on the **x-axis** of the graph?

....

b **Describe** what happens to the temperature of the water during the 40 minutes of Arun's experiment.

....

....

....

c **Explain** why the temperature of the water changes.

....

....

....

d The temperature of the room is 20°C. **Predict** what the temperature of the water will be at 50 minutes.

....

> 3.5 Ways of transferring thermal energy

Exercise 1

In this exercise, you will practise changing a verb into a noun. Then you will write a sentence using the noun.

Each of these verbs can be made into a noun by adding *-ion* to it. Sometimes, you have to change other letters in the word as well.

Write the noun that can be made from each verb. Then write a sentence that uses the noun.

The first one has been done for you. This is an unusual one, because the *b* in 'absorb' changes to a *p* in 'absorption'.

Verb	Noun ending with *-ion*	Sentence
absorb	absorption	In the Sun, black objects get hotter than white ones because their absorption of thermal energy is greater.
radiate		
convect		
insulate		
reflect		
conduct		

Exercise 2

This exercise gives you practice in using some of the vocabulary associated with scientific experiments. You can find information about this vocabulary in the English Skills and Support section.

Sofia predicted that hot water in a white can would cool down faster than hot water in a black can.

Sofia filled a black can and a white can with hot water.

She used a thermometer to measure the temperature of the water in each can, every five minutes.

black   white

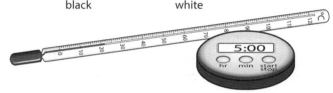

a List the **equipment** that Sofia used in her experiment.

   ....

   ....

b Write down the **hypothesis** that Sofia tested with her experiment.

   ....

   ....

c Sofia did a **risk assessment** before she began her experiment.
   Suggest one **risk** that Sofia should consider.

   ....

After 20 minutes, the temperature of the water in the black container was lower than the temperature of the water in the white container.

Sofia decided that this showed that the black container lost thermal energy by radiation faster than the white container.

d What is Sofia's **conclusion**?

   ....

   ....

e What **evidence** did Sofia use to make her **conclusion**?

....

....

f Does the evidence **support** or **refute** Sofia's **prediction**?

....

....

> 3.6 Cooling by evaporation

Exercise 1

In this exercise, you will choose the best phrase to complete a sentence.

Here are some phrases about cooling by evaporation.

Use the phrases to complete the sentences.

the change of state from liquid to gas   **escape into the air**
to allow water to evaporate from its surface   **is cooler than before**
the average kinetic energy of its particles

a Evaporation is ....

....

b The hotter a liquid, the greater ....

....

c A water cooler is made of porous clay ....

....

d When water evaporates, the particles with the greatest energy ....

....

e The water left behind after the most energetic particles escape ....

....

Exercise 2

This exercise is about using appropriate words to describe the results of an experiment.

Marcus prepared two boiling tubes like this.

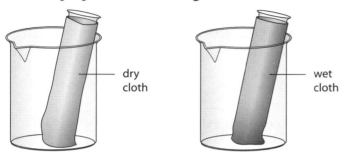

dry cloth

wet cloth

Marcus poured hot water into both tubes. He measured the temperature in the tubes every 5 minutes for 25 minutes.

The table shows his results.

Time in minutes	Temperature in °C	
	water in tube with dry cloth	water in tube with wet cloth
0	80	80
5	71	68
10	64	58
15	59	50
20	54	43
25	52	39

a Describe the **trend** in the results for the water in the tube surrounded by the dry cloth.

....

....

....

b What **pattern** can you see in the differences between the results for the water surrounded by the dry cloth and the water surrounded by the wet cloth?

....

....

....

c Make a **prediction** of the temperature in each tube at 30 minutes.

....

....

d Suggest how Marcus could change his experiment, to make his data more **reliable**.

....

....

e Marcus wants to check that the temperatures he reads on the thermometer are **accurate**. His teacher tells him that taking the same reading with two different thermometers will help him to do this. Is his teacher correct?

Explain your answer.

....

....

....

4 Maintaining life

> 4.1 Plants and water

Exercise 1

In this exercise, you will choose the best prepositions to complete sentences.

Choose a preposition to fill each of the gaps in the sentences. Sometimes, more than one preposition may work, so just choose the one you think is best. Choose from the list.

between   in   into   of   through

a   Water is taken .... a plant ....
its root hairs.

b   Root hairs grow .... the particles in soil.

c   Xylem vessels are found .... the centre of a root.

d   Water is transported .... xylem vessels.

e   The wood in a tree trunk is made up .... xylem vessels.

Exercise 2

In this exercise, you will write questions that match the answers.

Here are some answers to questions. Write a question that matches each answer.

Write your question twice. The first time, use a question word such as 'What' or 'Why'. The second time, use a command word such as 'Name', 'State', 'Describe' or 'Explain'.

The first one has been done for you.

Answer: Xylem vessels.

Question with question word: What do we call the tubes that transport water in a plant?

Question with command word: Name the tubes that transport water in a plant.

a *Answer*: Through root hairs.

Question with question word: ....

....

Question with command word: ....

....

b *Answer*: They are arranged in a circle near the outer edge of a stem.

Question with question word: ....

....

Question with command word: ....

....

c *Answer*: Mineral salts such as nitrate and magnesium.

Question with question word: ....

....

Question with command word: ....

....

d *Answer*: They are completely empty inside, and their end walls have broken down.

Question with question word: ....

....

Question with command word: ....

....

> 4.2 Transpiration

Exercise 1

This exercise will help you to check that you understand transpiration, as well as some of the vocabulary that we use to describe it.

In each of these sentences about transpiration, one of the words is incorrect.

Identify the incorrect word, and <u>underline</u> it. Then rewrite the sentence correctly.

Here is an example.

<u>More</u> water is lost from the top of the leaf than the underside.

Less water is lost from the top of the leaf than the underside.

a   Water diffuses from the inside of a leaf to the air in the form of a liquid.

....

....

b   Transpiration is the loss of water vapour from the roots of a plant.

....

....

c   A waxy layer on the underside of a leaf helps to reduce water loss.

....

....

d   Water moves out of leaves through the xylem.

....

....

e   Many desert plants have small leaves to reduce the rate of photosynthesis.

....

....

Exercise 2

> This exercise is about some of the vocabulary that we use when collecting, displaying and analysing the results of an experiment. Look at the *Language of science experiments* information in the English Skills and Support section to help you to answer the questions.

Arun took two very similar plants growing in pots. He covered the leaves of one of the plants with a thin layer of Vaseline. He did nothing to the leaves of the other plant.

Arun measured the mass of both plants. He left them both in the same place.

He measured their masses each day for the next five days.

The graph shows Arun's results.

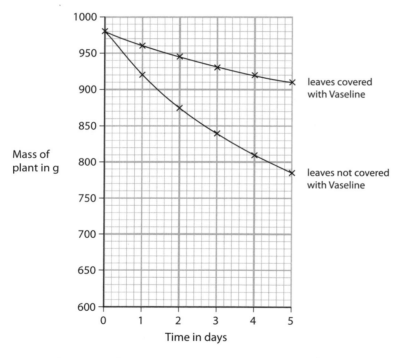

a What was the **variable** that Arun changed in his experiment?

....

b What are the **units** in which Arun measured the mass of the plants?

....

c **Describe** the **trend** shown by the mass of the plant without any Vaseline on its leaves.

....

....

....

d **Calculate** how much mass the plant with Vaseline on its leaves lost during the experiment.

....

e **Explain** why one of the plants lost more mass than the other one.
Use the word 'transpiration' in your answer.

....

....

....

....

....

f Arun wants to improve the **reliability** of his results.
What is the best thing for him to do? Tick (✓) one box.

display his results as a bar chart instead of a line graph ☐

do the experiment again, using six plants instead of two ☐

use a different kind of balance to measure the mass of the plants ☐

make a careful risk assessment before he does his experiment ☐

> 4.3 Excretion in humans

Exercise 1

> In this exercise, you will check that you understand how excretion happens, and that you can use the vocabulary associated with this topic.

Two words in each of these sentences have swapped places.

In each sentence, <u>underline</u> the two words that are in the wrong place.
Then write the sentence with the words in their correct places.

a Urea is made in the kidneys and excreted by the liver.

....

....

b The urethra carries urine away from the kidneys, and the ureter carries urine away from the bladder.

....

....

c Urea is a solution of urine dissolved in water.

....

....

d Urea is transported in the kidneys to the blood.

....

....

Exercise 2

In this exercise, you will write questions based on statements about the excretory system.

Change each statement into at least one question. Write more than one question if you can, but try not to ask anything that cannot be answered by reading the statement.

a *Statement*: The word 'renal' means 'to do with the kidneys'.

Questions: ....

....

....

....

b *Statement*: The ureters carry urine from the kidneys to the bladder, where it is stored.

Questions: ....

....

....

....

c *Statement*: The kidneys filter the blood and remove urea from it.

Questions: ....

....

....

....

d *Statement*: The excretory system contains several organs, including the kidneys, ureters, urethra and bladder.

Questions: ....

....

....

....

> 4.4 Keeping a fetus healthy

Exercise 1

> This exercise is about modal verbs. Look at the information about *modal verbs* in the English Skills and Support section to help you to answer these questions.

Complete each sentence, using the words that you think fit best.

Choose from the list.

> **can   cannot   must   must not**
>
> **should   should not**

a   A pregnant woman .... smoke cigarettes.

b   A pregnant woman .... eat foods containing plenty of iron.

c   Nicotine in the mother's blood .... get into the fetus's blood.

d   Some drugs, such as antibiotics, ... be good for health.

e   A pregnant woman .... take any drugs without consulting her doctor.

Exercise 2

> In this exercise, you will use phrases to write sentences about how a mother can take care of her health, and the health of her fetus.

Use each of the phrases to write a sentence about how a mother can keep herself and her fetus healthy.

a   *Phrase*: diffuses into the fetus's blood

    Sentence: ....

    ....

b   *Phrase*: to make haemoglobin

    Sentence: ....

    ....

c   *Phrase*: supplied by its mother's blood

    Sentence: ....

    ....

d   *Phrase*: extra calcium is needed

    Sentence: ....

    ....

e   *Phrase*: carbon monoxide, nicotine and tar

    Sentence: ....

    ....

5 Reactivity

> 5.1 Reactivity and displacement reactions

Exercise 1

In this exercise, you will choose the best prepositions to complete sentences. You may like to look at the reactivity series in Topic 5.1 in the Learner's Book as you answer these questions.

Each of these sentences contains at least one incorrect preposition.

Identify the incorrect preposition and <u>underline</u> it.

Then rewrite the sentence including a correct preposition. Here are some that you might find useful – but feel free to choose a different one if you think it works.

at	between	by	from	in	of	onto	to

a   A more reactive metal can displace a less reactive one into its salt.

   ....

b   Calcium is in sodium and magnesium in the reactivity series.

   ....

c   The word equation shows the reaction at zinc and hydrochloric acid.

   ....

d   If we put an iron nail into copper sulfate solution, the nail becomes coated onto copper.

   ....

   ....

e   The most reactive metals are written in the top of the activity series.

   ....

Exercise 2

This exercise will help you to check that you understand the reactivity series, as well as some of the vocabulary that we use to describe it. You may like to look at the reactivity series in Topic 5.1 in the Learner's Book as you answer these questions.

In each of these sentences about reactivity and displacement reactions, two of the words have swapped places.

Identify the two words and <u>underline</u> them. Then rewrite the sentence correctly.

Here is an example.

A change in <u>reaction</u> tells us that a chemical <u>colour</u> has taken place.

A change in colour tells us that a chemical reaction has taken place.

a Iron is higher in the reactivity series than potassium.

....

b In a displacement reaction, zinc will displace calcium from its salt.

....

c If a zinc nail is placed into copper sulfate solution, there is no reaction because copper is less reactive than zinc.

....

d Acids near the top of the reactivity series react violently with metals.

....

....

e Magnesium cannot displace silver from magnesium sulfate.

....

....

> 5.2 Using the reactivity series and displacement reactions

Exercise 1

This exercise is about some of the vocabulary that we use when doing experiments. Look at the *Language of science experiments* information in the English Skills and Support section to help you to answer the questions.

Sofia heated some copper oxide with powdered carbon sprinkled on top of it. The diagram shows the equipment that she used.

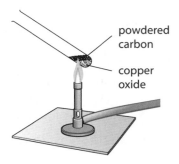

powdered carbon

copper oxide

a Name at least three pieces of equipment that are shown in the diagram.

....

....

b Sofia did a **risk assessment** before she began her experiment. State one risk that she should be aware of, and describe what she should do to stay safe.

risk: ....

staying safe: ....

....

Sofia let the hot tube and its contents cool down. Then she tipped them into a beaker of cold water. She saw little pieces of dark metal falling to the bottom of the beaker. She thought that this must be copper, which had been displaced from the copper oxide by the carbon.

c   What was Sofia's **observation**?

....

....

d   What was Sofia's **conclusion**?

....

....

e   Write an **explanation** for Sofia's results.

....

....

....

Exercise 2

In this exercise, you will write questions that match the answers.

Here are some answers to questions. Write a question that matches each answer.

If you like, you can use a question word such as 'What' or 'Why'.
Or, if you prefer, you can use a command word such as 'Name', 'State', 'Describe' or 'Explain'.

The first one has been done for you.

Answer: molten iron

Question with question word: What is produced when iron oxide and aluminium react in the thermite reaction?

Question with command word: State what is produced when iron oxide and aluminium react in the thermite reaction.

a *Answer*: Displacement reaction.

....

....

....

b *Answer*: To extract a metal from its ore.

....

....

....

c *Answer*: It is heated with carbon in a blast furnace.

....

....

....

› 5.3 Salts

Exercise 1

> This exercise will help you to check that you understand some of the vocabulary that you have used in this topic.

In each of these sentences about salts, one of the words is incorrect.

Identify the incorrect word and <u>underline</u> it. Then rewrite the sentence correctly.

Here is an example.

Salts formed from hydrochloric acid are called <u>chlorines</u>.

Salts formed from hydrochloric acid are called chlorides.

a The compounds present in sodium chloride are sodium and chlorine.

....

....

b Copper sulfate can be made by reacting copper oxide with hydrochloric acid.

....

....

c To obtain crystals of the salt, we can heat a solution of the salt we have made in an evaporating funnel.

....

....

d One way of making a salt is to add a metal to water.

....

....

e Nitrates are acids that can be made by reacting a metal with nitric acid.

....

....

Exercise 2

This exercise checks that you can remember and spell some of the words you need when you write about making salts.

Each of these statements describes a single word. Write the word that is being described. Make sure that you spell the word correctly.

a salts that are made from citric acid ....

b the process of forming crystals from a solution of

a salt ....

c a group of letters, and sometimes also numbers, that tells us which elements

are found in a compound ....

d an element that is contained in all acids ....

e the liquid that passes through filter paper ....

> 5.4 Other ways of making salts

Exercise 1

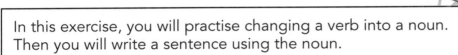

In this exercise, you will practise changing a verb into a noun.
Then you will write a sentence using the noun.

Each of these verbs can be made into a noun by adding *-ion* to it. Sometimes, you have to change or add other letters in the word as well.

Write the noun that can be made from each verb. Then write a sentence that uses the noun.

The first one has been done for you.

Verb	Noun ending with *-ion*	Sentence
react	reaction	A salt can be formed by the reaction between a metal and an acid.
crystallise		
neutralise		
erode		
filter		
evaporate		

Exercise 2

In this exercise, you must find the correct word to fit into a sentence.
To do this, you will need to understand how to make salts, and also how
the words in the sentence fit together.

Complete these sentences. Choose from the list.

alkali   calcium   copper   dissolve   excess

filter   filtrate   extra   sodium   water

Limestone is made from .... carbonate. When carbonates, such

as limestone, react with acids, a salt, carbon dioxide and .... are

produced. This can happen when acidic rain falls onto limestone rocks.

We can make .... chloride by adding copper carbonate to

hydrochloric acid, until some of the copper salt is left in the bottom of the beaker.

This is called using .... copper carbonate. When the reaction has

finished, we can .... the mixture to obtain a ....

containing .... chloride dissolved in water.

> 5.5 Rearranging atoms

Exercise 1

This exercise is about using connecting words to link two ideas together.

Complete each sentence, using these connecting words or phrases.

and   because   because of   but   in order to   so

a   When magnesium burns in air, magnesium .... oxygen react
to form magnesium oxide.

b   We know that the total mass of the products will be the same as the total mass
of the reactants, ... the law of conservation of mass.

c   The reactants must be heated .... provide energy to make them react.

d   The reaction between potassium and water is exothermic, ...
the reaction between sodium hydrogencarbonate and citric acid is endothermic.

e   The reaction is endothermic .... more energy is needed to
break the bonds than is released when new bonds form.

Exercise 2

> In this exercise, you will use phrases to write sentences about how atoms
> are rearranged in chemical reactions.

Use each of the phrases in a sentence about chemical reactions. You may need to
use the phrase at the beginning, in the middle or at the end of the sentence. Try to
write a sentence that includes information about what happens in chemical reactions.

Here is an example.

> *Phrase*: no new elements are formed
>
> *Sentence*: When a chemical reaction takes place, no new elements are formed.

a   *Phrase*: when magnesium is heated in air

   Sentence: ....

   ....

b   *Phrase*: of the reactants and the products is the same

   Sentence: ....

   ....

c   *Phrase*: increases after heating because

   Sentence: ....

   ....

d   *Phrase*: the number of each kind of atom

   Sentence: ....

   ....

e   *Phrase*: because one of the products is a gas

   Sentence: ....

   ....

6 ▶ Sound and space

> 6.1 Loudness and pitch of sound

Exercise 1

In this exercise, you will practise the correct use of some of the new vocabulary in this topic. You will also need to think carefully about the structure of sentences.

Here are some sentences about sound. There is something wrong with each sentence. You can make the sentence correct by changing either of two words.

Decide what is wrong, and <u>underline</u> the two words that can be changed to make it correct. Then rewrite the sentence in **two** ways to make two correct sentences.

Here is an example.

Sounds get <u>louder</u> when the distance from the source of the sound is <u>greater</u>.

Sounds get quieter when the distance from the source of the sound is greater.

Sounds get louder when the distance from the source of the sound is smaller.

a The greater the amplitude of a sound, the higher its pitch.

....

....

....

b The faster the vibration, the lower the pitch of a sound.

....

....

....

c The loudness of a sound depends on its frequency.

....

....

....

Exercise 2

This exercise checks that you can remember and spell some of the words you need when you write about the loudness and pitch of sound.

Each of these statements describes a single word. Write the word that is being described. Make sure that you spell the word correctly.

a a piece of equipment that we can use to see a waveform on a screen

....

b the distance from 0 to the top of a peak, or the bottom of a trough, of a wave

....

c the number of vibrations per second, usually measured in hertz

....

d a back-and-forth movement that produces a sound ....

e how high or low a sound is on a musical scale; it is affected by the frequency

of vibrations ....

> 6.2 Interference of sound

Exercise 1

This exercise asks you think about the word 'analogy'. You can find information about this word in the English Skills and Support section. You will also practise using some of the vocabulary that you have learnt in this topic.

We can use water waves as an **analogy** to help us to think about sound waves.

a Explain why this is a useful analogy.

....

....

....

b Describe **one** similarity and **one** difference between water waves and sound waves.

Similarity: ....

....

Difference: ....

....

c State what happens to the amplitude of a wave when two waves **reinforce** one another.

....

d Two waves meet so that the peaks of one wave exactly match the troughs of the other wave. Underline the word that describes what the two waves do to each other.

amplitude   **cancel**   **increase**   **reinforce**

Exercise 2

This exercise is about modal verbs. Look at the information about *modal verbs* in the English Skills and Support section to help you to answer these questions.

Complete each sentence, using the words that you think fit best.

Choose from the list.

can   cannot   must   must not   should   should not

a   Water waves .... interfere with sound waves.

b   Two waves .... only reinforce when they meet with their peaks and troughs together.

c   If the same sound is coming from two speakers, the sound waves

.... either reinforce or cancel each other at different points in the room.

d   Arun says that he .... hear anything, because his noise-cancelling headphones cancel out the sound.

e   If we want to reinforce a sound wave with a frequency of 450 Hz,

we .... use another sound wave with the same frequency.

f   Now write a sentence of your own, using one of the words from the list that you have not used in your other answers. Your sentence must be about sound.

....

....

....

> 6.3 Formation of the Moon

Exercise 1

In this exercise, you will use an active verb to rewrite a sentence about how scientists think the Moon was formed. Look at the information about *active and passive verbs* in the English Skills and Support section.

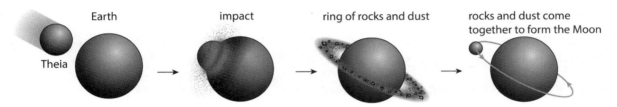

Earth   impact   ring of rocks and dust   rocks and dust come together to form the Moon

Theia

Each of these sentences includes a passive verb.

<u>Underline</u> the passive verb. Then rewrite the sentence using an active verb. You may also need to change some other words in the sentence so that it makes sense.

Here is an example.

Rocks <u>were sent</u> flying into space when the collision happened.

The collision sent rocks flying into space.

a   Dust and rocks were pulled together by gravity.

....

b   The Moon was formed from rocks from an object called Theia.

....

....

c   Rocks from the Moon were analysed by scientists.

....

d   It was suggested in the early twentieth century that the Moon was formed by splitting away from the Earth.

....

....

e   This idea was not confirmed by the calculations.

....

Exercise 2

In this exercise, you will write questions that match the answers.

Here are some answers to questions. Write a question that matches each answer.

You can use a question word such as 'What' or 'Why'. Or, if you prefer, you can use a command word such as 'Name', 'State', 'Describe' or 'Explain'.

The first one has been done for you.

> *Answer*: Collision theory.
>
> *Question with question word*: What is the name for the theory about how we think the Moon was formed?
>
> *Question with command word*: Name the theory about how we think the Moon was formed.

a *Answer*: Theia.

....

....

....

b *Answer*: The composition of their rocks is the same.

....

....

....

c *Answer*: It is less dense.

....

....

....

> 6.4 Nebulae

Exercise 1

> This exercise will help you to check that you understand nebulae, as well as some of the vocabulary that we use to write about them.

In each of these sentences about nebulae, two of the words have swapped places.

Identify the two words and <u>underline</u> them. Then rewrite the sentence correctly.

Here is an example.

> We can see the <u>northern</u> nebula from the <u>Orion</u> hemisphere.
>
> We can see the Orion nebula from the northern hemisphere.

a The plural of nebulae is nebula.

....

b Nurseries can be stellar nebulae.

....

c A cloud is a nebula of dust and gas.

....

d Gravity pulls stars of dust together to form clouds.

....

e A galaxy is a collection of dust, but a nebula is a collection of stars.

....

....

Exercise 2

In this exercise, you will choose the best prepositions to complete sentences.

Choose a preposition to fill each of the gaps in the sentences. Sometimes, more than one preposition may work, so just choose the one you think is best. Choose from the list.

at   between   from   in   of   than   to   without

a   One difference .... a nebula and galaxy is that a nebula does not contain mature stars.

b   Many nebulae are more than 10 000 times bigger .... the Solar System.

c   New stars are formed .... stellar nurseries.

d   We can see some nebulae .... a telescope.

e   The most common gases .... nebulae are hydrogen and helium.

7 ▶ Genes and inheritance

> 7.1 Chromosomes, genes and DNA

Exercise 1

This exercise gives you practice in how to respond to different question words and command words.

Here are some incomplete questions and their answers.

Choose the best word to complete each question. Choose from the list.

	Describe	Explain	Name	State	What	Where	Which

a *Question*: .... are chromosomes found?

   Answer: In the nucleus of a cell.

b *Question*: .... the chemical that chromosomes are made of.

   Answer: DNA.

c *Question*: .... is smaller – a chromosome or a gene?

   Answer: A gene.

d *Question*: .... the number of chromosomes in a human cell.

   Answer: 46.

e *Question*: .... do genes do?

   Answer: Each gene helps to control a particular characteristic.

Exercise 2

In this exercise, you will use phrases to write sentences about genes, chromosomes and DNA.

Write a sentence that contains the phrases provided.

a   *Phrase*: contains many different genes

   Sentence: ....

   ....

b   *Phrase*: have different numbers of chromosomes

   Sentence: ....

   ....

c   *Phrase*: like a twisted ladder

   Sentence: ....

   ....

d   *Phrase*: different versions of the same gene

   Sentence: ....

   ....

e   *Phrase*: two copies of each chromosome

   Sentence: ....

   ....

› 7.2 Gametes and inheritance

Exercise 1

> This exercise is about comparative adjectives and adverbs. Look at the information on *comparative adjectives and adverbs* in the English Skills and Support section to help you to answer these questions.

Use a comparative adjective or a comparative adverb to complete each sentence.

a Sperm cells are .... than egg cells.

b The faster a sperm cell moves its tail, the .... it can swim.

c Gametes have .... chromosomes than other cells.

d An X chromosome is .... than a Y chromosome.

Exercise 2

> This exercise is about using connecting words to link two ideas together.

Complete each sentence, using these connecting words or phrases. You can use each word or phrase once, more than once or not at all.

because   because of   but   in order to   so

a A body cell has two copies of each chromosome, ...
gametes have only one.

b A zygote has two sets of chromosomes .... it is formed
when a sperm cell fuses with an egg cell.

c A sperm cell has a tail .... swim to an egg.

d A zygote with XY chromosomes develops into a boy ....
one with XX chromosomes develops into a girl.

e There are equal numbers of sperm cells containing an X chromosome or a

Y chromosome .... there is an equal chance that a baby
will be a boy or a girl.

> 7.3 Variation

Exercise 1

In this exercise, you must choose the best prepositions to complete sentences.

Choose a preposition to fill each of the gaps in the sentences. Sometimes, more than one preposition may work, so just choose the one you think is best. Choose from the list. You do not have to use all of the words in the list.

at   between   by   from   in   into   of   than   to   within

a   There is variation .... the height of the people in my class.

b   Variation means the differences .... individuals belonging
to the same species.

c   Variation is caused .... genetic differences and also
the environment.

d   Not all variation .... a species is caused by differences
in DNA.

e   These leaves are divided .... several small leaflets.

Exercise 2

In this exercise, you will practise changing a verb into a noun.
Then you will write a sentence using the noun.

Each of the verbs in the table can be made into a noun, by adding either **-ion** or **-ment**. Sometimes, you have to change or add other letters in the word as well.

Write the noun that can be made from each verb. Then write a sentence that uses the noun. You can use either a singular or plural form of your noun. Try to make your sentence relate to the ideas you have met in this unit.

The first one has been done for you.

Verb	Noun ending with *-ion* or *-ment*	Sentence
move	movement	The movement of these two horses is different, because one has longer legs than the other.
vary		
fertilise		
combine		
measure		

> 7.4 Natural selection

Exercise 1

> This exercise will help you to check that you understand some of the vocabulary that you have used in this topic.

In each of these sentences about selection, one of the words is incorrect.

Identify the incorrect word and <u>underline</u> it. Then rewrite the sentence correctly.

Here is an example.

> Natural selection is a scientific <u>hypothesis</u>.
>
> Natural selection is a scientific theory.

a Advantageous features decrease the chance that an individual will survive and reproduce.

....

....

b Natural selection causes changes in a species over a very short period of time.

....

....

c Antibiotic resistance in people is caused by natural selection.

....

....

d Natural selection is less likely to cause change in a species if there is a change in the environment.

....

....

e Natural selection can cause change over time if there are no genetic differences in a species.

....

....

Exercise 2

In this exercise, you will practise turning statements into questions.

Change each statement into **one** question. Use a command word in your question, such as 'Name', 'State', 'Describe' or 'Explain'.

The first one has been done for you.

Statement: Natural selection can cause genetic changes in a species over time.

Question: Name the process that can cause genetic changes in a species to happen over time.

a   *Statement*: Natural selection can only happen when there is variation in a species that is caused by genetic differences between the individuals.

Question: ....

....

b   *Statement*: An organism that has an advantageous feature is more likely to survive long enough to be able to reproduce.

Question: ....

....

c   *Statement*: Natural selection has produced populations of bacteria that are resistant to antibiotics.

Question: ....

....

d   *Statement*: Varieties of genes that make an organism better adapted to its environment are more likely to be passed on to the next generation.

Question: ....

....

8 ▶ Rates of reaction

> 8.1 Measuring the rate of reaction

Exercise 1

> This exercise gives you practice in using suitable language when drawing
> and interpreting graphs.

Zara added magnesium to hydrochloric acid. Every 30 seconds, she measured the
volume of hydrogen gas produced. The graph shows her results.

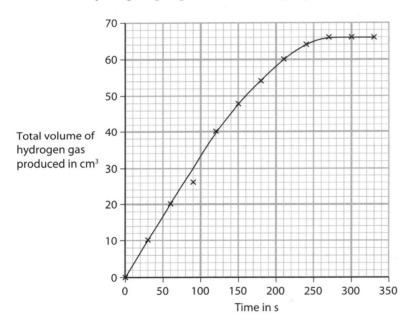

Complete the sentences. Choose from the list. You can use each word or phrase once or not at all.

> anomalous   axis   dependent   finished   gradient   increased
> independent   rate   sixty-five cm³   unreliable   zero

In Zara's experiment, the total volume of hydrogen gas produced is the

.... variable.

The .... of the graph tells Zara how quickly the magnesium and
hydrochloric acid are reacting together. This is called the .... of
reaction.

Zara ignored one of the points when she drew the line, because she decided the result was

....

Zara's graph shows that, after 270 s, the volume of hydrogen gas produced per minute

was .... This is because the reaction had ....

Exercise 2

In this exercise, you will practise using appropriate prepositions.

Choose a preposition to fill each of the gaps in the sentences. Sometimes, more
than one preposition may work, so just choose the one you think is best.

a   The rate of reaction is usually fastest .... the start.

b   We can measure the rate of reaction between a metal and acid by

     measuring the volume of gas produced .... a particular

     length .... time.

c   The steepness .... the graph tells us how quickly the reaction is happening.

d   We can collect the gas given off .... attaching a gas syringe

     .... the top .... the flask.

e   Another way of measuring the volume of gas is to collect it

     .... water in a measuring cylinder.

f   Now think of a preposition that you have **not** used in your other answers.

     Write a sentence about measuring rate of reaction that includes your chosen preposition.

     ....

     ....

     ....

> 8.2 Surface area and the rate of reaction

Exercise 1

In this exercise, you will think of a suitable comparative word to complete the sentences about the reaction between calcium carbonate and hydrochloric acid.

Complete each sentence, using a suitable word of your own choice.

a   The smaller the pieces the calcium carbonate are cut into, the .... their surface area.

b   The greater the surface area of the pieces of calcium carbonate, the

.... the frequency of collisions with hydrochloric acid particles.

c   The lower the frequency of collisions, the .... the rate of reaction.

d   The slower the rate of reaction, the .... it will take for all the calcium carbonate to disappear.

e   The closer we get to the end of the reaction, the .... the rate at which carbon dioxide is produced.

Exercise 2

In this exercise, you will check that you can use the correct names for pieces of scientific apparatus, and describe what they are used for.

The diagrams show three methods for measuring the quantity of gas produced in a reaction.

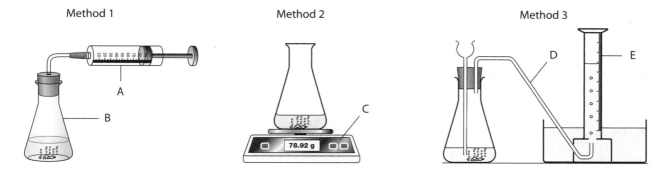

Method 1   Method 2   Method 3

a Name the apparatus labelled **A**, **B**, **C**, **D** and **E**. Choose from the list.

balance   beaker   conical flask   cup   delivery tube

gas syringe   measuring cylinder   measuring tube   pipe   timer

A ....

B ....

C ....

D ....

E ....

b Which method or methods measure the mass of the gas produced?

....

c Which method or methods measure the volume of the gas produced?

....

d Name one other measuring instrument you would need, to measure the rate of production of the gas using any of these methods. ....

> 8.3 Temperature and the rate of reaction

Exercise 1

In this exercise, you practise using the vocabulary needed to write about rate of reaction and temperature.

Complete the sentences. Choose from the list.

after   before   collide   cooling   decrease   heating

increase   less   more   precipitate   the same

a   When the temperature of the reactants is increased, the particles

.... more often.

b   If the mass of the reactants is the same, but the temperature is lower,

the total volume of gas produced when the reaction has finished will be

....

c   Preliminary work is done .... we carry out the experiment.

d   We can decrease the kinetic energy of the water particles by ....

the water.

e   We can measure how much carbon dioxide is produced by measuring the

.... in mass of the flask.

Exercise 2

This exercise gives you practice in writing about predictions.

Complete each sentence by making a prediction. There are often several different predictions you could make. Choose just one.

Here is an example.

If Marcus heats the hydrochloric acid, the kinetic energy of the particles will increase.

a   If hydrochloric acid is mixed with sodium thiosulfate, a precipitate ....

....

b   If the hydrochloric acid is hotter, the rate of formation of ....

....

c   If Marcus carries out a trial run, he will ....

....

d   If he does a risk assessment, ...

....

e   If we want the frequency of collisions to be greater, ...

....

> 8.4 Concentration and the rate of reaction

Exercise 1

In this exercise, you will practise the correct use of some of the vocabulary used in this topic. You will also need to think carefully about the structure of sentences.

Here are some sentences about rate of reaction. There is something wrong with each sentence. You can make the sentence correct by changing either of two words.

Decide what is wrong, and <u>underline</u> the two words that can be changed to make it correct. Then rewrite the sentence in **two** ways, to make two correct sentences.

Here is an example.

The rate of reaction <u>increases</u> when the concentration of the acid is <u>less</u>.

The rate of reaction decreases when the concentration of the acid is less.

The rate of reaction increases when the concentration of the acid is more.

a   If more acid is dissolved in the same volume of water, the concentration of the acid is decreased.

....

....

....

b   When the concentration of the acid is greater, collisions between the acid particles and metal particles happen less frequently.

....

....

....

c   In a more concentrated solution, there are fewer particles in each cm^3.

....

....

....

Exercise 2

In this exercise, you will practise turning statements about rate of reaction into questions.

Change each statement into **one** question. Use a command word in your question, such as 'Name', 'State', 'Describe' or 'Explain'.

The first one has been done for you.

Statement: Increasing the concentration of reactants increases the rate of reaction.

Question: Describe what happens to the rate of reaction when the concentration of reactants is increased.

a *Statement*: We can make a more concentrated solution by dissolving more of the substance in less water.

Question: ....

....

b *Statement*: It increases because the particles collide more frequently when the concentration is greater.

Question: ....

....

c *Statement*: We can either record how much gas is made every 20 seconds, or we can time how long it takes to collect $30\,cm^3$ of gas.

Question: ....

....

Electricity

> 9.1 Parallel circuits

Exercise 1

This exercise will help you to check that you understand some of the vocabulary about circuits.

The diagrams show two electrical circuits.

Circuit 1

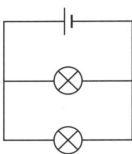

Circuit 2

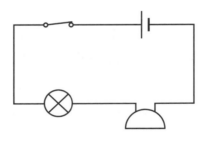

Complete the sentences. Choose from the list.

ammeters   branches   cell   series   parallel   lamp

a   Circuits 1 and 2 both contain a ....

b   In circuit 1, the lamps are connected in ....

c   There are no .... in a circuit that is connected in series.

d   In a .... circuit, a gap anywhere in the circuit stops the

current flowing in all parts of the circuit.

e   The current divides in a .... circuit.

Exercise 2

In this exercise, you will use modal verbs to write about what happens in a parallel circuit.

The diagram shows a parallel circuit.

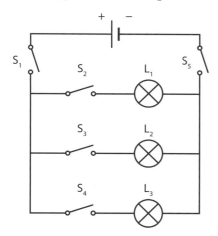

Complete the sentences about the circuit in the diagram.

Choose a suitable modal verb from the list.

can   cannot   must   must not

a   In this circuit, the current .... follow more than one path.

b   For any of the three lamps to light, switches S_1 and S_5 ....
be closed.

c   If we want all three lamps to light, we .... close all
five switches.

d   If we want only lamp L_1 to light, we .... close switches
S_3 and S_4.

e   If one of the lamps breaks, the other two lamps .... light.

> 9.2 Current and voltage in parallel circuits

Exercise 1

> In this exercise, you will check that you understand the vocabulary used when talking about current and voltage.

Choose the correct sentence endings for each sentence starter.

Copy the sentence endings carefully, with no spelling mistakes.

the units in which voltage is measured
a measure of the electrical energy in a circuit
connect a voltmeter in parallel with the lamp
connect an ammeter in series with the lamp

to measure voltage
the units in which current is measured
to measure current

a Volts are ....

   ....

b Amps, or amperes, are ....

   ....

c Voltage is ....

   ....

d We can use an ammeter ....

   ....

e We can use a voltmeter ....

   ....

f To measure the current in a lamp, we should ....

   ....

g To measure the voltage across a lamp, we should ....

   ....

Exercise 2

In this exercise, you will check that you can write the names of circuit components correctly.

Each of these symbols represents a component that is used in electrical circuits.

Write the name of each component next to the symbol. Make sure that you spell each name correctly.

a ....

b ....

c ....

d ....

e ....

f ....

g ....

> 9.3 Resistance

Exercise 1

In this exercise, you will practise the correct use of some of the vocabulary used in this topic. You will also need to think carefully about the structure of sentences.

Here are some sentences about resistance. There is something wrong with each sentence. You can make the sentence correct by changing either of two words.

Decide what is wrong, and <u>underline</u> the two words that can be changed to make it correct. Then rewrite the sentence in **two** ways, to make two correct sentences.

Here is an example.

The <u>thicker</u> the wire, the <u>greater</u> its resistance.

The thinner the wire, the greater its resistance.

The thicker the wire, the lower its resistance.

a The longer the wire, the lower its resistance.

....

....

....

b Resistance is measured in volts.

....

....

....

c In Ohm's law, the letter I represents resistance.

....

....

....

Exercise 2

In this exercise, you will use an active verb to rewrite a sentence about resistance. Look at the information about active and passive verbs in the English Skills and Support section.

Each of these sentences includes a passive verb.

<u>Underline</u> the passive verb. Then rewrite the sentence using an active verb. You may also need to change some other words in the sentence so that it makes sense.

Here is an example.

Resistance <u>can be calculated</u> by dividing the voltage by the current.

We can calculate resistance by dividing the voltage by the current.

a Resistance was studied by Georg Ohm.

....

....

b The thick wire was found by Arun to have a lower resistance than the thin wire.

....

....

c The results table can be used to calculate the resistance of the circuit component.

....

....

> 9.4 Practical circuits

Exercise 1

In this exercise, you will practise using sentences to describe a circuit.

Look at each circuit diagram carefully. Then describe the circuit in words.

Here is an example.

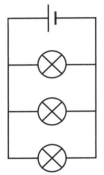

This is a parallel circuit. It has three lamps, each on a separate branch of the circuit. It has one cell.

a

....

....

....

b

....

....

....

c

....

....

....

Exercise 2

In this exercise, you will use comparative words to describe changes in circuits.

The diagram shows a circuit that includes a variable resistor.

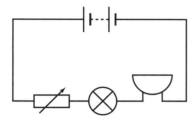

Use a comparative word of your own choice to complete each sentence.

a   When we increase the resistance of the variable resistor, the current in the

circuit becomes ....

b   The lower the current in the circuit, the .... the lamp.

c   A .... current flowing through the lamp makes it shine
more brightly.

d   When we decrease the resistance, the lamp is ....

e   It is much .... to change the brightness of the lamp if we
use a variable resistor instead of a fixed resistor.

⟩ Acknowledgements

The authors and publishers acknowledge the following sources of copyright material and are grateful for the permissions granted. While every effort has been made, it has not always been possible to identify the sources of all the material used, or to trace all copyright holders. If any omissions are brought to our notice, we will be happy to include the appropriate acknowledgements on reprinting.

Thanks to the following for permission to reproduce images:

Cover Stephan Geist/EyeEm/GI; Inside **Unit 1** Stephan Geist/GI; Tonnaja/GI; **Unit 2** Jack0m/GI; **Unit 3** Georgeclerk/GI; Zoonar rf/GI; Golfbress/GI; Imagenavi/GI; **Unit 4** Electravk/GI; **Unit 6** DougSchneiderphoto/GI; Bryan Allen/GI; **Unit 7** Dole08/GI; Gk Hart/Vikki Hart/GI; **Unit 8** SDI Productions/GI; **Unit 9** FatCamera/GI

Key: GI= Getty Images